Wishing you a Christmas

of jingling bells and bright spirits

To

Sammie

From

Grama Suzie

2009

Jingle Bells

Jingle Bells

ILLUSTRATED BY

Michael Hague

Henry Holt and Company

NEW YORK

Dashing through the snow,
in a one-horse open sleigh,

O'er the fields we go,
laughing all the way.

Bells on bobtail ring,
making spirits bright.

Oh, what fun it is to sing a sleighing song tonight!

Oh! Jingle bells! Jingle bells! Jingle all the way!

Oh, what fun it is to ride
in a one-horse open sleigh, hey!

Jingle bells! Jingle bells!
Jingle all the way!

Oh, what fun it is to ride
in a one-horse open sleigh!

Published by Henry Holt and Company, Inc., 115 West 18th Street, New York, New York 10011.
Published in Canada by Fitzhenry & Whiteside Limited, 195 Allstate Parkway, Markham, Ontario L3R 4T8.

Library of Congress Cataloging-in-Publication Data
Hague, Michael
Jingle Bells / illustrated by Michael Hague.
Composed by James Pierpont in 1850 and first published in 1857.
Summary: An illustrated version of the famous Christmas song.
ISBN 0-8050-1413-6
1. Christmas music. 2. Children's songs. [1. Christmas music. 2. Songs]
I. Pierpoint, James, 1822–1893. II. Title.
PZ8.3.H119351990
782.42'1723—dc20   90-32066

Henry Holt books are available at special discounts for bulk purchases for sales promotions, premiums, fund-raising,
or educational use. Special editions or book excerpts can also be created to specification. For details
contact: Special Sales Director, Henry Holt & Co., Inc., 115 West 18th Street, New York, New York 10011.

First Edition | Designed by Marc Cheshire
Printed in the United States of America
Recognizing the importance of preserving the written word,
Henry Holt and Company, Inc., by policy, prints all
of its first editions on acid-free paper.

1 3 5 7 9 10 8 6 4 2